Where I Come From

Poems by Jackie Warren-Moore

All rights reserved. No poem or artwork may be reproduced in full or in part without prior written permission from its owner.

Copyright © 2016 by Jackie Warren-Moore

ISBN-10:   0-9976147-3-0

ISBN-13:   978-0-9976147-3-2

First edition.

Nine Mile Press
4451 Cherry Valley Turnpike
LaFayette, NY 13084

Nine Mile Press is an imprint of Nine Mile Art Corp. See the complete list of our books and magazine publications at www.ninemile.org

Many thanks to the Central New York Community Foundation, Inc., whose generous grant made the publication of this book possible.

Acknowledgements

Some of these poems have been or will be published, as follows:

"On leaving Auburn Prison," *Born into a Felony*, ed. Walt Shepperd and Stewart Brisby, PulpArtForms, 1978

"Daughters," *Sisterfire: Black Womanist Fiction and Poetry*, ed. Charlotte Watson-Sherman, Harper Collins, 1994

"Daughters," "For The Children," "For Paula Cooper," and "Death Wish," *Writing Our Way Out of the Dark: An Anthology by Child Abuse Survivors*, ed. Elizabeth Claman, Queen of Swords Press, 1995

"For Paula Cooper," "For Etheridge Knight," "Dannamora Contraband," "The All Night Issus," *Spirit and Flame: An Anthology of Contemporary African Ameican Poetry*, ed. Keith Gilyard, Syracuse University Press, 1997

"For Etheridge Knight," "Ego Food," "Double Take for Andy," *Passionate Lives*, ed. Elizabeth Claman, Queen of Swords Press, 1998

"Games," "Unlocking Midlife," *Age Ain't Nothing But A Number: Black Women Explore Midlife*, ed Carleen Brice, Beacon Press, 2003 and published internationally by Souvenir Press, London, England, 2005

"The Speaking Lesson," *Growing Up Girl: An Anthology of Voices from Marginalized Spaces*, ed Michelle Sewell, Girlchild Press 2006

"She Wears Red," "Yes, The Body Remembers," *The 100 Best - African American Poems *But I Cheated*, ed Nikki Giovanni, Sourcebooks Media Fusion, 2010

"Dashed Hopes," *Stone Canoe*, Syracuse University Press 2011

Some of these poems have also been previously published in *Jackie Warren-Moore: Greatest Hits 1980-2003* (Pudding House Press, 2004).

Contents

Foreward	7
On the Occasion Of The Passing of Civility	13
Dear Brother Martin	14
She Wears Red	16
Games	18
Daughters (All Four Of Them)	20
Blue Flame Of My Anger	21
Following The Lead Of A Young Magician	22
Would Be King	24
The Message	25
Horseplay	26
If Ever	27
To The Poet In The Top Hat	28
Ms. Mean	29
Untitled	30
I Am A Kite	31
Death Wish	32
If	33
For Etheridge Knight	34
Ego Food	36
Double Take	37
Unlocking Midlife	38
Starlight	39
Yes The Body Remembers	40
Where I Come From	42
Portrait Of Thelma	43
The Weight Of The World	44
Tightrope	46
I Am Trayvon	47
Brown Tree Bent Or Post Surgery Blues	48

Dannemora Contraband	49
Too Deep In The Funk	50
Mouth	51
Tonight	52
Going Places	54
Brown Skin Service	56
Oswego Blue 1	57
18th Anniversary	58
The Women Gather	60
Dream Stealers	61
Recipe For Forgiveness	62
Blue Sea Gift	63
What I Gather	64
About Jackie Warren-Moore	67

Foreword

I come from a long line of women who are speakers. Women who planted their feet firmly on Mother Earth and spoke out. Women who have spoken out to praise and sustain what was right in their world. Women who balled their fists, prepared for battle, and screamed out against injustice.

I was destined to be a speaker. My history, my family, my own sense of placement in the world would not let me shirk the job. My Grandmother, Louise Lee, an Ancestor I never had the opportunity to meet, set the tone. From all accounts she was a big, bold woman with strong opinions. GrandMa Louise was prohibited by her family from marrying my Grandfather, Harry Lee, back around 1915, because he was "too dark." She planted her feet, covered every inch she stood on, and made her own decision. My Mother, Leta Mae Lee, was born from that decision.

If any doubt remained regarding my own destiny, the events of a Summer evening in 1970 dispelled it. My Mother and I were driving through a well-known strip of bars and restaurants on the Syracuse University Campus. As we passed one of the more popular night spots, we saw that a crowd had gathered. At the center of the crowd lay a young Black man. His body lay in the road with his neck pressed against the curb as if it was a pillow under him. A tall young White man stood with his foot pressed down on the man's neck. Three or four other young White men urged the one to "break his neck."

My Mother's reaction was immediate. She slammed on the brakes, threw the car in park, and simply said: "Come on." She got out of the car and opened the trunk, reached in, and pulled out two tire irons. She handed one to me. She raised her tire iron to her shoulder and quickly stepped into the crowd. I held mine tightly and followed.

My Mother demanded that the young White man back off and release the Black man. The crowd was silent. The man looked at the two of us. Perhaps he was surprised to see two tire-iron wielding

Black women or perhaps they were surprised to hear someone voice an objection to what they were about to do. Whatever they thought, the man removed his foot. The Black man, my Mother, and I moved slowly back to the car. As we drove away from the staring crowd my Mother laughed and said, "That was a close one."

She began to talk to the young man about the ways Black people had to survive in those trying times as she drove him home. I sat in the back seat shaking. It was then that I knew that I could not "make my mark" in the world in the same way that was second nature to my Mother. I admired my Mother for her guts, strength, and wisdom. I wanted to imitate the way she served the community. I realized my weapon of choice was words. I have been writing ever since.

To shut my mouth and sit silently by, as some would have me do, is to suffer many deaths. I choose life, and must therefore speak. As Audre Lorde, noted Poet/Sister/Ancestor has said: "Your silence will not save you." And even Helen Keller, another woman who might have been silenced, tells us: "Life is either a daring adventure or nothing at all."

So I speak. I speak about what I see, and what I feel and do as a Black woman in today's world. I try to make connections, the connection that honest words of communication are capable of between listening hearts. I believe poetry cuts through all the societal B.S. that keeps human beings apart. My Mother used to tell me: "There are no new feelings under the sun." Beneath the skin, class, and lies that separate us, we are all the same. It is only open hearts, open hands, and communication that will connect and save us all. So I speak. I try to pass on the courage and the art of speaking to my Daughters, my Grandsons, Granddaughters, and anyone else who will listen.

There have been detractors, those who would have my big woman voice couched in their version of creative expression. I do not say that my words are any more valid than anyone else's but simply that they are my words and I dare to speak them in a society that otherwise may try to silence the likes of me.

    This book has been a long time coming. It contains both older and newer poems. Each poem has a life of its own. In preparing this manuscript I've had the opportunity to revisit every one of them again. It was quite a trip! I ran the gamut of emotions, not all of them pleasant, but all uniquely mine. I'm pleased to share them with you.

    I'd like to thank my Husband, Andy Moore, and my Daughters SonCeria, Andrea, Joi, Mia, for loving me despite myself. I'd like to thank my Grandchildren, Justin, Ramone, Nya, Laila, who take love to a new level.

    I'd like to thank the small circle of friends who know me and love me enough to let me be me.

    I'd like to thank the person reading my words and acknowledging where I come from.

Jackie Warren-Moore
Syracuse, NY 2016

Where I Come From

On The Occasion Of The Passing Of Civility

No please, no thank you
Excuse me, How can I help you?
No eye contact, beyond the cut of an eye
A sneer and the flip of the bird

We have lost each other
In a boiling sea of meanness and indifference
No kind words to connect us, no holding open the door
Holding out a neighborly hand to steady us

No touch of comfort or healing
We hit and run
Plunder and hide
The mean spirit of our rage

We have lost touch in the crush of humanity
The bleeding sore of our greed
We have lost it
The soft shoulder to lean on warmth of kindness

The healing of a simple smile
Affirmation of a Hello
We have lost it
Watched it stumble wounded and moaning
Into the abyss
We have lost the meaning of civility
In remembrance, respect and regret
Let us reach out our hands once more
And say simply, Welcome

Dear Brother Martin

I am writing this because the children asked me to
There is so much their young souls yearn for
They believe in the dream, believe you are looking
Lovingly down
They believe you have the knowledge and the power
They say your dream did not come true
Fruit of a charred lynching tree
Produces a bitter fruit and the children are hungry
Open mouths open minds yearn for the bittersweet taste of freedom
The children say you lead the way to the mountain top
We tried to follow but lost our way stumbling over hatred and
    ideology
Broken circle of trust yawning out — we left no crumbs to find our
    way home again
And so we wander, wander aimlessly and leaderless from one hate
    filled day to another
Blood dripping down every wall

Only in our bleeding are we united
Black blood, White blood, All blood, red and flowing
We are drowning in our own blood
The dream gurgling pink from our lips
Blood streaming down a child's face
Yet the children believe and look wide eyed and open handed
Into the glaring face of the future
They look to you, Martin, ask you
To beseech that Master you serve and send down a Spirit
Filled with vision
To pick up the mantle and command the river to rise
Rise river rise, fresh water dreams come flowing down
Down, down where we stand, stand, stand

Rise river flow
Courage coursing through the ages gone by and come again
Rise mighty river, let the course of history overflow your banks
And saturate minds that thirst for the sweet taste of knowledge
Rise mighty river and flow, flow unobstructed and finally free

The children asked me to write this,
They tapped on my shoulder frantically, waved their small hands for
    my attention
And thrust this handful of words in my face
Write Martin they said, ask him again to point the way
Convene and close the circle
All hands united
All colors side by side
Shoulder to shoulder we stand
Flow like a mighty mighty river until
We are all finally free

She Wears Red

She bangs hard on the door
Just outside my consciousness
This wild woman I am becoming
"Let me in, open up," she screams
Wearing a long blue dress
Of dreams I discarded

I try to ignore her
Go about everyday duties
A list that must be followed
She keeps showing me new ways
To be me
Lessons I forgot
She wears red and says
She is staking a claim to beauty
Drops people like bad habits
Cutting hurt from her body
Carving a new switch to her step

"More bounce for the ounce," she says
"More cushion for the pushing"
She is a vulgar girl
Knows just what she wants
Throws her head back and laughs out loud

She is something
This new girl I almost was
"Open up," she says
"Be me again
The girl you were afraid of
Wear red again

Wear your hair down"
Black and grey hairs you earned
With the passion you stored inside
"Open up," she says, this wild woman I am becoming
"Open up," and welcome
This woman we are

Games

Nobody ever told me how fast the game was played
How it could end on the pump pump pump of a heartbeat
No one ever said that the days
Months years shoot by like comets
And become fixed
In a night sky constellation
You can only gaze at
Everybody neglected to say what each card meant
How it got dealt
The consequences of folding way too soon
Nobody put up signs
Nothing popped up
On all the right roads
Suddenly turned treacherous
Nobody ever told me lessons flew by
And I didn't take notes
Bogarted my way into the game
Bluffed my stuff

Parlayed my hand
Into a trump
I survived
Weaving and dodging
Running blindly
Steadily moving from
One card to the next
House full of cards
I prayed would never come tumbling
Down upon
My unbowed head
Nobody ever told me

You leave the game
With what you brought in
Held tight in your fist
In your heart
Butt naked and palm open
Nothing sticks
Everything falls away

Nobody ever told me
Love was the only right answer
To questions I didn't know to ask
Nobody ever told me
How it could all begin
On the pump pump pump
Of a heartbeat
Each beat
A new hand
Another chance
To begin
To love
To play the game

Daughters (All Four Of Them)

Red tipped triangle of the Ancestors
Misty guides support and urge me forward on dusty African trails
I move towards the twin peaks — green breast thrust to the sky
Traveling down, down, deeper down to the waiting valley between
The brook runs like glistening sweat between the globes.

I find myself there. Waiting and laughing. Holding hands with my
    daughter
Loving her as I never loved myself
Little girl laughter in threes
Old self
New self
Daughter.

We are three
We are one
Splashing water that falls in triangles against soft brown skin

Shadows form as I prepare to leave
I am reluctant to leave them there
We join hands — old self, new self, daughter
Red tipped triangle of the Ancestors skipping home

Blue Flame Of My Anger

Ignites
Nothing so ordinary
As red flaming passion
Blue, I tell you
Hot and scalding
Pouring flame
Consuming
Sticks to your skin
Burns blue
Charring from the inside out
Blue angry flame
Licking sadness
From the corner of my mouth
Blue flame of anger
Ignites

Following The Lead Of A Young Magician

For Ruth Forman

This poem gonna be the Mother, Father,
Grandmother poem of the week
Gonna be so cool, it freezes the July beef on city streets
Gonna be so real
Children of murder victims
Don't have to read the details in the morning newspaper
Gonna be so slammin'
Fifty Cent, gonna talk about makin' love not sex
Gonna be so vitamin enriched
Kids won't go to bed hungry
At the end of the month
Gonna be so fashion conscious
Kids can pay less
And walk tall
In any clothes they wear
Gonna be so gentle
Daddy won't beat Mama no more
While the kids watch

Gonna be so truthful
The government won't lie to the people
Who own it
Gonna be so brave
It's gonna shout the truth
About injustice
And the lives it devours
Gonna be so long
It wraps around
And strangles racism

In a hangmans noose
This poem is gonna be so spicy it spews
All the right words
To soothe wounded souls
Gonna be so educated
It makes smart bombs dumb
And disarms them
This poem gonna speak when I want to shout

This poem gonna be consciously peaceful
In a world of chaos
This poem gonna grow legs
And stand on its own
And speak
Speak
Speak

Would Be King

For Rufus Wiggins

I know why my mother loved you
At your best you are a brightly robed Dahomey King
Or at least his most trusted advisor
Night black skin stretched taut over muscle
As you peer at the sky
And calculate how many light years it would take
Your gold toothed smile to dim the sun
Damn near drunk and rubbery, slip sliding
With down home juke joint rhythm
Rhythm blue veined Northern Black ladies
Have been bred to forget
City slick, slow talking, honey dipped words
Your hand on your knife
Not a prize fighter, but a surprise fighter
A thick chunk of history, reminding me of fish and
Grits breakfasts of Southern Sundays I will never know
It is in remembering that I know why I love you

Note: Blue vein societies of the anti-bellum south admitted only Black people with skin light enough in color to see the blue of the vein.

The Message

In honor of Johnny "Jump Up" Chambers —10/21/90-2/24/07

All endings have beginnings and all beginnings have ends
Rewind the anger
Pull back the trigger
Before it explodes
Into everyone's life
After the anger and pain
After the death
After the blood
After the arrest
After the sentence
After all
All the destruction
To what end
End of life
End of love
End of all
All endings have beginnings
All beginnings don't end
In happiness
Or happy ever afters
Just part 2
Chasing
The sheer pain
Of Part 1

Horseplay

Part 2 Of The Message

Horseplay or play play
Or dying one day
So it begins
Hit and hit back
Hit and hit harder
Till the blood flows
And a whole string of "Sorry's"
Can't bring him back
Loss banging into my head
Exploding out of my heart
Horseplay or play play
Dying one day
Never a come back
From the meanness
Blood flowing from a Champions heart
Counting your last breath
Horseplay or play play
No way to tell when or what might explode

Violence spraying into your face
Death chattering
On the razor edge
Twirling a tech nine
In everybodies faces
Horse play or play play
Or dying one day
So it begins
Oh God, so it ends

If Ever

If ever I open the battle
Uncork the dream
Produce the drama
Free the genie
That hides inside
If ever I become
All that I contain
Unleash the passion
Warehoused within
If ever I write the whole story
Tell the whole sorry tale
If ever I dare
To own
Who I am
Say who I've become
Be who I wish
I will be free

To The Poet In The Top Hat

For Walt Shepperd, on his 65th birthday

To the Poet in the top hat and purple Converse's
Strutting his stuff in a slow drag of words with the power of a slam dunk
To the man who took me to Auburn prison and let me witness souls uncaged and set free with the power of their words and his belief in them
To the Poet who put UNIT in unity and made moves of peaceful politics and excellence way before it was politically correct and chic
To Lorca's Dad who made hamster homes in cozy closets he constructed with love
To the brother who recognized a sister in me and first celebrated my voice
To the friend who reached from the inside out to us born into a felony
To the Editor, word quick, with an already written obit in the bottom left hand desk drawer
To the Poet with the top hat and purple Converse's, a pocket full of poems on stash
Still young enough to warn you not to crowd him in the paint

Leading a parade
Making a way
Slam dunking the job on unit time
To the Poet in the top hat and purple Converse's
Making a difference

Ms. Mean

They call me mean
I'm not mean, just very self assured
They say I'm hard on furniture
Bustin' it up and tossin' it away
They say I'm hard on life
Ridin' it roughshod, right into the ground
They say I'm hard on men
Chewin' them up and spittin' out what's not real
They say I'm too heavy
Flesh heavy word heavy
I'll make a lightheaded man cry
They call me ugly, but my mirror keeps flashin' proud
They call me lazy, but I know what work best suits a Queen
They call me too much, but I see myself as just plenty
They call me too hot, too cold, too hard to hold
They keep trying to chip away — casting far flung adjectives and
    epitaphs
They call me lots of things

But most of them have never seen
A fully grown Black woman before

Untitled

New poems pop up like dandelions
Bright and persistent
My passion strewn bright yellow
Across the lawn
Deeply rooted and perennial
Summer long reminder
Of what I longed for
All the Winters of my life

I Am A Kite

I am a kite
Big bodied and fragile
Wind has taken me
Watch me shimmer with delight
Trembling everywhere I'm touched
In open air

I loop and bow low
Bend and very nearly break
For freedom
I am a kite
Harnessed wild thing
I soar
Unencumbered by what snatches me from sky
Tethered still
I strain to fly free
Whirling and gliding
A thingamajig

Unrivaled

I soar
Trembling with freedom's
Flying delight
Love me for what I am
I am a kite

Death Wish

For Uncle Joe

Had luck been with me, you would have died ten minutes
Before I met you
Your soft brown eyes and loving touch
Made me believe my father had come back from the dead
God had realized his mistake and returned him to me
You laughed with his laugh — the same spring brook chuckle
And all-encompassing hug

Yours was the first penis I had ever seen
Pulsing and purple — a demon unzipped
A drop of fluid at its eye/mouth
My ten year old mind not knowing if it was weeping or drooling
As it pointed accusingly at me
"Trust me" you said
"It's alright" speaking with my father's voice
All the wrongness of it whispered
In a voice I longed to hear

If only you hadn't held me with my long dead father's arms
If only I hadn't needed to be held so badly
If only I had known it was alright to wish you dead
If only it hadn't taken me twenty years to voice the shame of it
To speak of the not-all-rightness
If only you had died
Ten minutes before you forcibly
Entered my life

If

If teardrops were quarters and love was for sale
I'd be a very rich woman
If truth could see and I were God
I'd destroy the world and build again
Six days non-stop
If I were master and you were slave
I'd sacrifice a purified lamb
In the name of Allah
And all dead Saints
If chess were checkers
I'd surrender to your king and end the war
If life were free and came with a warranty
I'd give birth to 200 smiling Black babies
If too many teardrops didn't mean a flood
If being God didn't mean somebody on their knees
If being master didn't mean somebody being nigger
If surrender didn't mean after the battle

If being born didn't mean without warranty
As is
If
    If
        If

For Etheridge Knight

I learned of your death over spiced tea
With my breath blowing against
The thin membrane of the academic circle
The one constantly turning in on itself

I sat through polite and grammatically correct conversations
A full rundown of all your sins
Which actually killed you?
Heroin or cocaine?
Pussy or the lack thereof

Was it your last love or the old love
Newly found
That sheltered you
In the last shuddering moments
Heard them speak of the Tsk tsk trauma
Tragedy of a miserable life

Not one motherfucking mumbling word about the passion
About the lust for life that led
You crashing over the cliff
Like the soft brown baby boy you were

Not one note of the Coltrane riff that rode you
Through the long prison nights
Not one word of the copper thighs that wrapped you safe
From a world gone stir crazy
Not one stanza of the academic prosody
That sought to make you abandon the mother tongue
Not one motherfucking word about the bars
Etched indelibly in your mind

And mine
I suck your words
Roll them bitter across my tongue
And mourn my loss

Ego Food

They say you are what you eat
I've been told my lady fingers are delightfully cinnamon
I cry pure rock candy crystals
My toes are perfectly formed tootsie rolls
If you squeeze my tongue
It pours mandarin orange juice
I bleed red licorice juju beads
And whole handfuls of my thighs are sponge cake
Almond joy flows from my chocolate mound breasts
The inside of my ears makes raspberry jelly
And the column of my neck is a butterscotch lick
The walls of my womb drip pineapple juice in season
I sweat sugar water
And should you ever taste me
You'll know your sweet tooth has found a home

Double Take

For Andy

The next time I can't bear the sight of you
When I'm really pissed off and fantasize about
Scratching, kicking and biting out at you
When I feel at any moment
I'm going to threaten to call Peter the divorce lawyer
When I smile nastily while thinking of packing your
Twos and fews
And banishing you from my life

I'll take time
To remember
That sunny Fall day
The way the moist earth
Clung to your calloused fingers
As you plunged into the earth
To plant my flower bulbs

How you spoke friendly like
To the earth worm you disturbed
Picked him up and moved him gently
Out of the path of your task
I'll remember that your big clunky gentleness
Was one of the first things
That made me love you
I'll remember
And I'll smile

Unlocking Midlife

I'm collecting locks — deadbolts and hook eyes
Aching for the click click
Satisfied fit of the tumbler when the pieces fall into place
The puzzle piece
Gently, not jammed
Fits
And I see the picture for the first time
Understand the skeleton key
That fits every door even
If its not locked
Thrown open — the empty room beckons
And I spread my big body all around it
I lounge and get comfortable
Sprawl out and dream
Of other doors
Yet unopened

Starlight

Sometimes when I'm low
Even God thinks I'm a fool
Saying the same old, same old
    Star light-star bright
Dear God
Make him love me prayer
Night after night
Season after season — moon
Please make the closeness stay

Star bright-warm moon love
A galaxy is too far for this love to travel
Bright star blinking in an unseen universe,
Casting blinding light and no hope on a wishful thinking
Whispered love prayer
Sometimes when I'm low
Even God thinks I'm a fool

Yes The Body Remembers

Yes, the body remembers
When the brain wishes to forget
Thin snatch of song hummed
Up from the back of your past

The times they are changing
Or a certain whir in the atmosphere
The way the air hits the shin
A certain jig in the walk
A step that reminds us of all
We lost to time
Sickness and ignorance

The body remembers, all the way to the bone —
Pain
Pleasure
Etched into the marrow

Slick glide of time over lives
Connected by threads
We are too blind to see
Too sophisticated to acknowledge

The body remembers
Quick flash of tingle
In the back to synapse
Tiny pause — between conscious thought
Feelings surface
The body asserts
Come back, come back come back
To the feeling

Let the body remember
Feel again
All she has forgotten
All she continues
To hold onto
Yes, she remembers

Where I Come From

I am from Boogaloo blues
Backyard BBQ's
And too much booze
I am from Summer days beneath the same peach tree
I wished my step father hung from
Intoxicating smell of peach blossoms
Impending death at age 8
Filling my nostrils
I am from a time of waiting
Waiting for the world to change
Waiting to change the world
I am from back closet beatings
With leather belts rolled over ashy fists
I am from raised eye-hand clasped Catholic Mass
Crusted over welts on the back of my fat thighs
I am from screaming nights and broken bottles
I am from the shifting sands
Hands of step fathers I wish I never knew

I am from way deep sobs on Cardboard Hill
The world shifting beneath my feet
I am from ancient murderous thoughts and primitive fear
I am from Boogaloo blues
Back yard BBQ's
And too much booze

Portrait Of Thelma

Battle scarred and worn thin
Full of sad songs and blues
Tired and beaten down
By too many men, too many babies and just
Too too much
Too many that took and took from you
Left you numb and swaying in alcohol and disbelief
That life could slip by so fast while you stood swaying
Vague memories of what was once beautiful and important
You tell the sad sad story of one unknown bird
Lovely beyond description
Who sang one long trilling perfect note
Was silent
Sang no more

The Weight Of The World

Got up this morning
With a load of history on my back
Strapped down
As Sonia says: "My days not coming one at a time"
History making me
Limp along unfazed

I got history
Weighing me down
Keeping me earthbound
When every part of me
Wants to soar
Way beyond sinew and pain
Morphine haze and history
I'm trapped in
It ain't personal, it's political
And everything political
Is personal

And way past personally pathetic

It is a history gone wild
Inside my body and mind

Inside the Un-united States of America
It's a long line of days, seasons and years
With a burden on my back

It is a numbering of lessons
Still held in promise
Yet unborn

Rushing, striving to the tick tick tock of someone else's clock
Slow down/hurry up/get moving/deadline/get it done
Fast track/don't lay back/
Early rise/cook/clean/do something
Just move, girl
Clock striking
All the tick tocks in a row

Adding up to something left to be done
Step to step
Tick to tock
Don't stop
All hands pointing at me
Running from myself
Into myself
Hiding from myself
Sinking deeply into myself

I found myself on the edge
Fell head first into myself
Tumbled and turned
Stumbled and almost
Miss stepped
Danced myself open
Walked straight into myself
Became the woman I am

Tightrope

There are no slaves here
Only ignorance and prejudice
On a tightrope of hate
Murder waiting to happen

Whose sorrow is relevant to injustice?
Jealousy of those
Unequal or just us
Us who have waged
The battle worn
Stereotypes yet
Till our faces split
And pieces fall into
Place
Anger leaking bloodily through
Exposing the mask
We must face in the mirror

Just us who must make the revolution have meaning
Spin the world around
Crack the back
Of Intolerance
For all time
Break the tightrope
Of racial tension.

I Am Trayvon

I am Trayvon and the lines are blurred
Between life and death
Hope and madness
History and somebody else's damn story
Told all over again and again
Bloody and bloodier
Page after page
A history of shame and Blacks made to take the blame
I am slipping and sliding in the blood of our sons
The same old song and acquittal of crime
After crime, time after time

I am the Grandmother protector — tired of telling sons
To beware of the extra danger of being Black — Black feeling always
    under attack
Profiled and denied to death
No rest for the weary

Black Black
Feeling always under attack
Trayvon
No justice no peace
No rest
Just us who are left

Brown Tree Bent Or Post Surgery Blues

The tree browned and my back bent
Leaned over and said goodbye to pieces of me
Strewn along the way
This little piggy went to market
And never came home again
What foul sadness has been cut from me
My anguish carved out of the depth
Buckets of loss carted off
Catalogued
Floated past me in a haze
Don't take too much I prayed
My soul just past skin deep
Is mine to keep
Brown tree bent
Don't break
Lean over and say goodbye
To what life carted away

Dannemora Contraband

Stony lonesome reached out and grabbed me
Surrounded me with grey walls
Gun towers and fear
Dannemora blues made the clouds weep buckets on our heads
Inside, on the count where the youngbloods walk
With a warriors bounce the proud grey haired man
Speaks of the Ancestors and half
A century of long lonely nights inside
Inside Dannemora
Inside himself
Smiles weigh more in Dannemora
Inside a smile can soothe like a Mother's lullaby
Satisfy like a lover's caress
It can bandage a wound deep and festering
Touch the primal Ancestor in us all
Inside a smile can share what might be missed by the faceless
Passerby
To those men surrounded by grey walls

Gun towers and fear
When the clouds open and pour buckets
When the night wraps itself long and lonely around you
Listen carefully to the sound behind the raindrops
It is only me on the other side
Tossing smiles over the wall

Note: Dannemora is the general name for the Clinton Correctional Facility, a maximum security prison in Upstate New York. I conducted writing workshops there.

Too Deep In The Funk

Too deep in the funk to put some stink on it
Down way too low to even speak it
Too way down to have the bloody bones give voice to the pain
Seeping into the marrow
Shame of the dead leaf
On the otherwise vibrant tree of life
And love's longing
Too funky to drag out all the
Pointed fingers of blame
Was it poisoned or did it die
Of its own angry heart and heavy load of sadness
Such a loss!
Such a deep well of sadness
Too deep in the funk to put some stink on it
Too long gone

Mouth

Of course, I think about other parts of you
But it is always your mouth I come back to
Pink open and waiting to taste
You bring out the flavor in me
You come to me hungry
My pleasure is in filling you up
Our mouths pressed together
Lips crushed and swollen against mine
Caramel and purple
You bend to seek me out
A slow grind of purpose and texture
Such texture
I trace my fingers across your lips
Remember
No words
Just open mouthed longing
It is always your mouth
I come back to

Tonight

Tonight I am slow
Blue burn of jazz
Crushed half note
Spit in a can
Sadness bouncing from aluminum
Side to side

A pitiful sound
Lonely unused and no need to recognize
Recycle gun metal song unsung
A sax note
Snatched in a calloused hand
Crushed before it was allowed to soar

Tonight I am so slow
Blue burn of jazz
Newly invented
Older than dream

Of sphinx
Blue note
Caught in my throat
Death rattle or someone else's song
So slow   so slow
    Blue burn
Record playing
Over and over
        In my mind
Worn out scratch
        Of loneliness
                Loneliness

All up   and down
Down
    Down
        Down
The scale

Going Places

First you took my mind
Made me wet
Came stealing out of the blue night
Pulled up my anchor
All the feeling come tumbling down
Flowing like the river you tamed
Inside me
Touched me
Stroked me
Wet wild woman
Beneath your commanding fingers
Ordered me to come to you
And I came
Tumbling down to the well where the pleasure
Springs from
Found the lost one
In the little boat
Rode it rocking

Thrashing to shore
First you took me
Into your hands
Molded me into the shape
That fit you best
Rolling ride to pleasure
You took me
Where I always wanted to go
I went wet and willingly
Into your pliant fingers
Dipped in the honey of me

First you took my mind
Made me wet

Brown Skin Service

Sometimes you make me feel like a service station
You pull in sleek, Black shiny with your motor humming
I rush out in uniform to service you with a smile
Fill you up with high octane, put a tigress in your tank
Clean your windows so you can see where you've been and just where
    you are heading
Change your oil, flushing out all the impurities
Fine tuning you with the most advanced techniques
Torque your engine and put new fire in your plugs
Adjust your timing for the long haul
Sometimes you make me feel like a service station
Brown skin service with a smile
And I'm the only business in town

Oswego Blue 1

It is boiling
This sea I am
Waves break hard against
Shores that have stood
Times test
Shores pile up
In spite of me
It is boiling
This sea I am
Vast and blue wide
Shy birds can't land here
Remains untamed
Threatening to spew
Over borders and landmarks
That have come before
Return with all the seas might
Refuse to be contained
Passion spews straight up

From the depths of this
Boiling sea I am
Heavy droplets in
Sun danced sea air
Making new patterns
From age old
Deep
Not still water
It is boiling
This woman sea I am

18th Anniversary

Maybe
It happened in Summer
And I only imagine it happened in Fall
When the colors grow brilliant
Catch the eye
When the beauty pulls me
To shapes and shades of life
Just before
They wither and die
Like the one inside
So briefly I felt you
Long before your first flutter
I sent you away
To some spot
I've never known
You left me bloody
Repentant and sorrowful
Praying

That you would make the journey
Again
Come back to me
When I was wise enough
To open and embrace you
Love you like the almost child
You were
Colorful
Shape and shade
Of life
Just before

Maybe
It happened in Summer
And I only imagine
It happened in Fall

The Women Gather

I am a soft jingle
In a roomful of sisters
All flavors
Nana, mother, sister, woman
The determined one
Child of God
One lost on the way to being found
One missing
In the half dozen voices
The chorus we are becoming
I am a soft jingle
In a room charged with life
A circle of sisters speaking
The women gather in circles
Looking outward
Preparations
Kneaded like soft baked bread
By warm dark hands
Flung like the sun's rays

The women gather in circles
Rainbow colored and tightly knotted
Weaving magic and shaking the air
Our voices raised and mingling
A satisfied sigh against heaving brown breasts
The women gather in circles
Swaying in unison
Speaking in rhythm
Making plans to rock the world

Dream Stealers

Dashed hopes and dreams
Litter the street
Broken pieces of promise
Sparkling
Once whole
Crunch beneath us

Dreams
Fragile as butterfly wings
Smudged into nothingness
In mid-flight

Oh, you dreamers
Guard those visions
Precious and rare
Dream stealers abound
Sniffing the air

Recipe For Forgiveness

First be the pain
Open wide
Take the ache into your mouth
Roll it across your tongue
Feel the heat
Sting of sadness
Stink of bitterness
Let the anger sink deep
Into your bones
Roll with the pain
Rock with it all night long
Wrap your arms around it
Wrestle it till dawn
Then
Arch your back
Open up
Face to the sky
And let it go

Blue Sea Gift

"Sky, water, eyes of the man in the tree," he says
Images claim and reclaim me
Over and over calling
Girl, in blue sea
Swimming against the tide
Take this wave
Rolling and free foaming
Ride it warm
Enveloping into sea called destiny
These are your images
No matter how many
Times you disclaim them
They are yours
Mother earth woman
You are
Sky, water, eyes of the man in the tree

Claim them

Hide them behind
Cool blue sea water
Of dreams
No longer young
Girl in blue sea
Swimming yet
Against the tide

What I Gather

What I gather becomes me
All air
Blue sky Blue tree Blue rock
Ache for blue sea
Big bodied woman
I swallow the world
What pain moves through me
I watch the dragonfly from earth
How I wish to soar
Dance like a darning needle in sky
Slow drag of winds whisper
What joy moves through me
Blue blur of wings
Dance in warm evening air
What I gather becomes me

I take it in
Let it flow around
Through me
Passing
Only sorrow falls away

About Jackie Warren-Moore

Jackie Warren-Moore is a poet, playwright, theatrical director, teacher, and freelance writer, whose work has been published nationally and internationally. She is, as she has said, a Survivor, who has survived racism, sexism, sexual abuse, and physical abuse. She regards her poetic voice as the roadmap of her survival, a way of healing herself and of speaking to the souls of others. She has said, "I believe I have an obligation to speak up and celebrate what is right in the world and to shout out about what is wrong in the world, in the hopes that we may all work together to make it right for us all." Ms. Warren-Moore makes her home in Syracuse, NY.